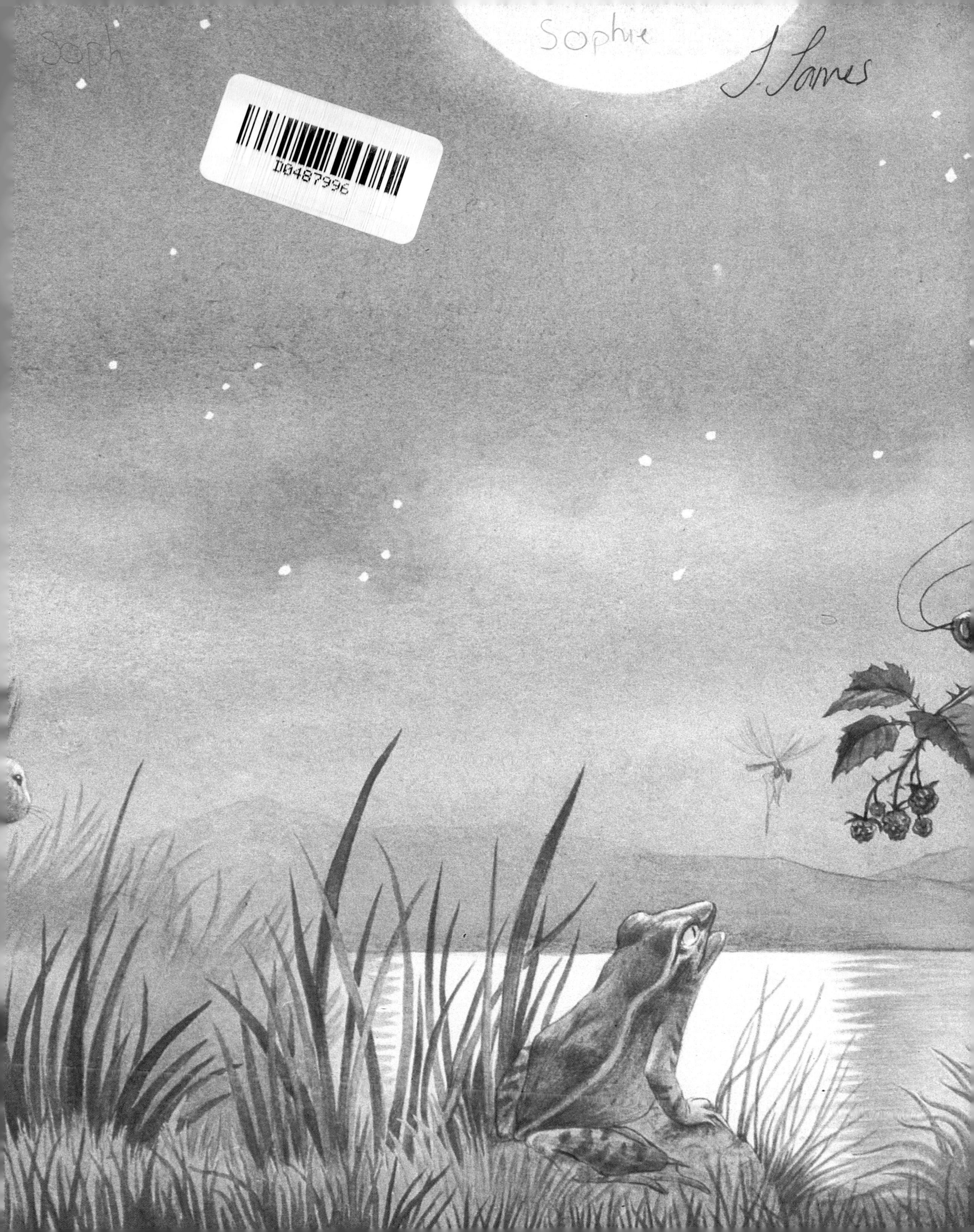

WRITTEN BY

GAUD MOREL AND DORINE BARBEY,
ALEXANDRE M. CZAJKOWSKI, MARIE FARRE,
ANNE DE HENNING, CHRISTINE LAZIER,
PIERRE PFEFFER, NATHALIE TORDJMAN

ILLUSTRATED BY

NICOLE BARON, LAURA BOUR, BERNARD DAGAN,
PIERRE DENIEUIL, LUC FAVREAU, MONIQUE FELIX, DONALD GRANT,
PIERRE DE HUGO, CYRIL LEPAGNOL, ANNE LOGVINOFF, PHILIPPE MARLE,
AGNES MATHIEU, RENE METTLER, DANIEL MOIGNOT,
SYLVAINE PEROLS, JEAN-MARIE POISSENOT, PASCAL ROBIN,
JACQUES ROZIER AND MONIQUE GAUDRIAULT,
FRANK STEPHAN, DOMINIQUE THIBAULT,
GRAHAM UNDERHILL, DIZ WALLIS

TRANSLATED AND ADAPTED BY

CLARE BEST AND SIMONA SIDERI
WITH SARAH MATTHEWS, SARAH GIBSON,
PENNY STANLEY-BAKER AND SUE BIRCHENALL

We gratefully acknowledge the advice of:
Jane Ostler,
Simon Pryce, B.Sc., F. Arbor.A
Bill Matthews, Men of the Trees,
Sarah Heath, M. Phil Conservation Policy,
John Howson, Education Officer, Friends of the Earth
Cover design by Peter Bennett

ISBN 1 85103 180 4
© 1990 by Editions Gallimard
English text © 1993
by Moonlight Publishing Ltd
First published in Great Britain 1993 by Moonlight Publishing Ltd,
36 Stratford Road, London W8
Printed in Italy by Editoriale Libraria

EXPLORING NATURE

CONTENTS

MOONLIGHT PUBLISHING

There are many different habitats on our planet.

You won't see the same kinds of plants and animals all over the world. Each has its natural habitat*. The plants and animals which live together and share a habitat form an ecosystem*. At the Equator it is hot and steamy – vast rainforests cover the land. Towards the Poles the weather gets cooler and cooler, until the climate is so bitter no trees grow. In between lie many other habitats – temperate regions, deserts, mountains, rivers, seas...

Most of Europe has a temperate climate. It is never too cold, too wet, or too dry.

The taiga where this thrush lives is a huge conifer forest stretching across Siberia and parts of Canada.

Plants and animals have adapted* to climate.
Over millions of years they have changed to survive in different sorts of conditions. Conifers, like spruce and pine for example, grow high in the mountains. They can develop in the cold, even if few animals can endure it.

The baobab and acacia trees of the African savanna lose their leaves in the dry season to survive the drought. The plant-eating animals that roam the plains have to travel long distances in search of food and water. In the rainforest there are no seasons and the climate is the same all year round, so trees keep their leaves.

Long grasses cover the savanna. Few trees can grow where there is such a short rainy season.

They vary according to the climate and the soil.

Similar ecosystems* occur all over the world, wherever similar conditions exist.

The temperate zone includes much of Europe and North America, as well as parts of South America and Australia.

The trees of the rainforest grow very tall and many have huge leaves.

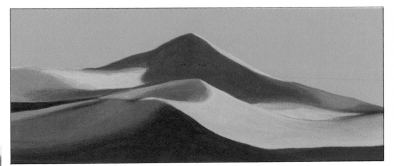

Not all deserts are hot and sandy, like in the picture above. They can be cold, mountainous and rocky.

Temperate regions support mixed forests of evergreen conifers and deciduous* trees. Near the Equator are rainforests. Subtropical forests or savanna thrive in places where it is not so hot and wet. The cold climates of the Arctic tundra or high mountains have their own ecosystems. There are deserts where no rain falls. In each ecosystem the plants and animals that live there must be able to survive the conditions.

The icy wind that sweeps across the tundra destroys all living things, apart from the odd bush and a few stunted trees.

- High mountains and tundra
- Temperate forest and conifer forest (taiga)
- Steppes and prairies (temperate dry plains)
- Mediterranean and subtropical vegetation
- Deserts
- Savanna (hot dry plains)
- Rainforest

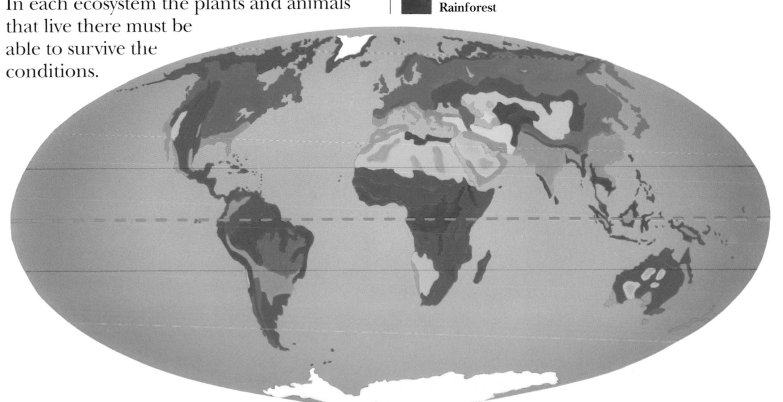

The forest is growing all the time.

In a temperate climate, such as that of Europe and North America, most of the trees are deciduous* and lose their leaves each autumn. Long ago the land was all covered by forest. But people needed space to plant crops and pasture animals, so the trees had to be cut down. Now in some places there aren't any trees left at all.

If an acorn lands on soft earth it produces a small root and a shoot. Soon the first two leaves appear.

At 3 years old the seedlings are about 30 centimetres high. They have buds, bark and a spindly trunk.

By the time they are 10 years old the oak trees are between 1 and 3 metres tall. They grow close together in a thicket.

How does the forest grow?

A single oak may produce thousands of acorns, but only a handful of them will ever grow into trees. There is not enough space, light or water to support all of them. The weaker ones die.

Many European woods have been managed for centuries, with woodmen looking after the trees and cutting them down at the right time. This encourages the forest as a whole to grow strong and healthy.

These tall, slim oaks are 50 years old.

Oaks are fully grown or mature at 100 to 200 years old.

The life of a tree

Count the numbers of rings in the sawn-off trunk to learn a tree's age.

A tree grows all its life.

The trunk is made of rings of light and dark wood. Every year a new ring forms just under the bark – one for each year of the tree's life. In spring, buds and shoots grow and the branches and trunk of the tree become longer and thicker. If the tree isn't cut down or blown down in a storm it will live for hundreds of years.

When a branch breaks off, insects creep into the wound to lay their eggs. Long threads of fungi enter the wood and help break it up. Slowly the tree will rot and die.

In a managed wood foresters try to grow as many good trees as they can by planting new ones, clearing away weeds and dead branches, thinning out weaker trees and checking constantly for pests and diseases.

The older an oak tree is, the more birds and animals make their homes in it. Can you name them all? Notice the many different fungi living on the tree.

The plants and animals of the forest...

Daffodils

Wood anemones

Lesser celandine

Common dog-violet

Moss, fungi, snowdrops, bluebells and primroses grow in the thick carpet of dead leaves and twigs. They come out in spring, before any leaves appear on the trees and block out the light.

Pheasants strut through the undergrowth, while a rustle of leaves may be a bank vole scuttling for cover. In France or Spain you might even see wild boar or a striped fire salamander, as in the picture below.

...are all part of the food chain.

Boletus • Ink Cap • Field mushroom • Chanterelle

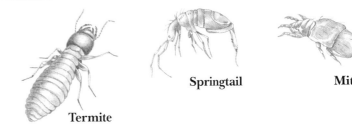

Termite • Springtail • Mite

The plants and animals that live in the forest need each other to survive.

They form a close community* in which each has an important job. Together with the climate and the soil type they create the delicate balance we call an ecosystem*.

If you look down at the ground you will see

pebbles, bits of old leaves and twigs all mixed up together: this is the leaf litter. Underneath is the top-soil. It is dark brown, and full of goodness. Digging deeper the ground becomes light and soft and a bit damp. Here the roots of plants and bushes spread out, looking for food and water.

Soil is made up of tiny particles of stone worn away over millions of years from solid rocks. In the water around the particles are the minerals* that all plants need for food. But how does the ground stay rich and full of goodness when so many plants and animals draw their food from it?

The leaf litter feeds the whole forest.

It is home to thousands of tiny insects which you can't see without a magnifying glass. They feed on the leaves that fall in autumn and dead wood that drops to the ground. In the rain the leaves and twigs soften. Tiny creatures, known as bacteria*, digest them and break the dead matter down into humus*. This is a natural fertilizer which feeds the soil and provides minerals for the plants.

Earthworm

Other creatures like slugs, snails, millipedes and woodlice also live in the soil and amongst the leaf litter. They eat seeds and roots, insect eggs and other minute animals.

Earthworms play a central part in the upkeep of the soil. They turn over the earth letting air in and drag fallen leaves underground where they start rotting. Their body wastes provide food for the soil. Have you any idea how many earthworms you could expect to find in a one acre field? About 2 million!

As day breaks, the wood comes alive.

Have you ever been to the woods early in the morning? If you go, find a good hiding place and keep very still. You may hear a woodpecker drilling at the bark of a tree, or see a nuthatch scampering down the trunk head first. They are looking for insects to eat. Deer may appear, nibbling at fresh, young shoots or you might spot a fox skulking in the undergrowth, waiting for a bird or a rabbit.

Robins build their nests from dead leaves low in the tangled undergrowth.

Plants and insects, herbivores* and carnivores* all have their place in the forest food chain*.

You won't see a lynx in Britain. It lives in the forests of North America, though a few are still left in the mountains of continental Europe.

A stag beetle with its antlers raised, a pine marten about to pounce, an eagle owl, a boar, a stag and two does, a fox chasing a hare and a badger looking for food

Many animals come out at night.

Hares come out into clearings. Badgers leave their setts and follow old paths in search of worms and insects to eat.

Owls hoot and seconds later swoop down on voles or shrews.

Hedgehogs uncurl and totter off on spindly legs in search of grubs and berries.

In German forests you might spot a wild boar rooting among the leaves for insects.

A herbivore*, like a woodmouse, feeds on nuts, berries or leaves. It will be eaten by a small carnivore*, such as a weasel or fox, which in turn may be killed by a larger carnivore. Some animals, like foxes, will be killed by people using guns or traps.

The woodcock builds her nest on the ground. She is well camouflaged* amongst the leaves.

Forest foods, woodland crafts

The outer bark of the cork tree is peeled off every twenty years to make cork for bottles, floats for fishing lines and buoys.

Since earliest times the forest has provided us with many useful things.

Prehistoric people collected wood to make fires. They ate berries from the trees and made medicines from the roots and leaves of many plants.

In the Middle Ages, pigs were left to forage under the trees in autumn, when the nuts had fallen. If the harvest was bad, people gathered chestnuts and acorns to eat.

Today herb teas are a favourite drink and we still collect blackberries and hazelnuts in autumn.

If you go for a walk in the woods, don't fill your pockets with berries, nuts and mushrooms. Remember, some of them are poisonous!

Check with an adult what is safe to pick.

Don't forget that the animals need to eat too. And the forest itself needs its seeds and dead leaves to grow healthy and strong.

Pine resin or sap was used to make paints and varnishes.

Today we use synthetic products instead so resin is no longer harvested.

Charcoal was made by packing small logs tightly together in a very hot oven with little air. It was used in blast furnaces and for smelting iron. It has been replaced by coke.

Wild strawberries

Buckthorn

Chanterelle

Wood Mushroom

Morel

Sweet chestnuts

Hazel nuts

Bilberry bush

The sap from pine trees was collected in buckets placed under a notch made in the bark.

Is wood used in your home?

Doors, window frames and kitchen units are often made of pine. The paper in your exercise books was probably pulped from Norway spruces. Wood can also be processed. Some wood extracts are used in medicines, others are mixed with plastics to make building materials.

Woodmen and foresters care for the forest.

Trees grow slowly and before cutting them down the woodmen have to be sure the forest will continue to be fruitful.

You may see coppices in a managed forest. The trees have been cut back at ground level and allowed to produce many shoots. The new branches grow slender and straight and are ideal for walking sticks, fencing and light building materials.

But not all forests are properly managed. Fewer trees may be replanted than are felled. Look out for wood products which come from sustainable* sources. If fast-growing conifers are planted where deciduous* trees have been cut down, the original forest animals will not be able to live amongst the new trees and will either move away or die.

Woodmen use chain saws to fell the trees and lop off their branches.

The trunks are taken to the sawmill where they are cut into planks. The wood must dry out, or be seasoned, before it can be used.

Young trees are kept in a nursery for two to three years, and then planted out in evenly spaced rows.

A coppice provides shelter for many animals and plants, as well as being an excellent source of wood.

Redwood forests, eucalyptus forests, tropical rainforests

Each forest is a different habitat*.

The forest ecosystem* will vary according to the climate, the altitude and the soil type. In Europe, there are conifer forests and mixed forests, each with its own character and with a different balance of wildlife. In California there are forests of giant sequoias or redwoods, the biggest trees in the world.

Sequoias are named after a Cherokee chief who first wrote down his people's language. The Sequoia National Park was created in 1890 to protect groves of these trees which are amongst the world's oldest living things.

Pandas live in the bamboo forests of China. They love to feast on young shoots.

The rainforest is dense and impenetrable.

At least that's what most people think. In fact, there are lots of different types of rainforest.

The aerial roots of the banyan tree help to prop it up.

What they have in common is that the trees are tall evergreens. There may be more than a hundred different species* of trees in a small area. The Amazon rainforest is quite dark. A canopy of enormous leaves keeps out the sunlight. Little undergrowth can survive so the forest floor is clear. In subtropical forests more light penetrates and the ground is a tangle of plants. You need a machete to cut a path through it!

In Australia, koalas live high up in tall eucalyptus trees of which there are about 600 different species.

All over the world forests are at risk.

Oak, beech and sweet chestnut trees grow in temperate forests. They lose their leaves in autumn.

Mediterranean countries are hot and dry. Many trees have small leathery leaves which fall, a few at a time, throughout the year.

Forests are vital to life on Earth.

Trees produce oxygen* and take in carbon dioxide, cleansing the air. They protect the soil against erosion*.

Each year thousands of acres of forest go up in flames. It takes the land many years to recover after such damage.

Forests are destroyed to make way for homes and roads.

The forest canopy shelters the ground from the sun and from heavy rain, and tree roots collect the water in the ground preventing both flooding and drought.

Young trees are planted to replace those cut down, but water can flow between neat rows of trees, causing flooding and erosion.

Never play with fire in the woods!

If you make a fire or have a barbecue, be sure you keep to the places allowed for this. An adult should be in charge. Don't leave litter: it can start a fire in hot sun.

Where fire is a danger, broad strips of land called fire breaks are stripped of vegetation to stop the fire spreading. There may be look-out towers as well.

Hedges planted and tended by people...

Have you ever followed the line of a hedge on a walk in the country? A hedge is a narrow strip of bushy shrubs and trees, such as hawthorn, dividing one piece of land from another. In the country, wild flowers, birds and small mammals make the hedge their home. The hedge, with all its inhabitants, is called a hedgerow.

In Britain and northern Europe, hedges border roads and rivers and cross farmland and heath. Without hedges, the landscape would be dull and bare. Hedges are not only beautiful, they are useful in all sorts of different ways.

Many hedgerow plants and animals could not survive out in the open. The hedgerow protects them from harsh weather. We can gather nuts and berries, firewood and mushrooms from hedgerows.

Hedgerow trees or bushes growing beside a river put down roots which stop the water washing away the banks.

Hedges help us to look after the land.

They keep farm animals in, and unwanted animals out. They give animals shade in summer. Because their roots absorb a lot of water, they help prevent flooding. The hedge stops soil being washed away in heavy rain, or eroded* by dry winds.

You can get some idea of the age of a hedge by counting the different types of shrubs and trees in it. The more types there are, the older the hedge is. A hedge with more than five separate species* could be several hundred years old. A hedge with ten species might date back to Saxon times.

Hedges around houses keep out the wind and the noise of passing cars. They add a welcome splash of green and a fresh scent of their own.

Hedges need our care and attention if they are to work well. Trees and bushes must be trimmed and smothering plants removed.

Box and yew hedges in formal gardens are sometimes clipped into special shapes. This is called topiary.

The hedger used to weave lower branches into the gaps in the hedge or cut and lay main pieces along the bottom. This made the hedge dense or bushy.

Nowadays people often put up barbed wire or fences across gaps instead. Many animals, birds and insects will die of starvation or cold whenever a hedge is pulled up or allowed to die.

One fifth of Britain's hedges have been removed since 1946. Now farmers are encouraged to restore and replant hedges.

Years after destroying a hedgerow, the farmer may realize just how important it was. But a new hedge takes years to grow.

In the south of France people plant rows of cypress trees to keep out the strong mistral wind.

As years go by, hedgerows grow and change. You can see how a hedgerow changes as season gives way to season.

The hedger uses a billhook to cut back branches. Most hedge-cutting is now done by machines which tear the plants.

The hedgerow comes alive in spring.

Birds raid the hedgerows for twigs, moss and strands of animal hair to line their nests.

In April the sap begins to rise.
It comes up from the roots, bringing fresh life to the tip of every twig.

Blossom appears early in the shelter of the hedgerow. Tiny white flowers cover the blackthorn for about ten days, then wither as the first leaves unfurl.

As the days grow warmer, the grass snake comes out of hiding and sets off in search of birds' eggs to eat

A few toadstools begin to sprout among the violets at the foot of the hedge. Snails appear, clinging to the underside of new leaves.

The long-tailed tit may make its nest among the dense growth of the hedge.

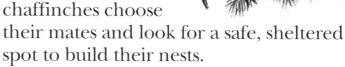

There are more hours of daylight and the air is full of birdsong. Hedge sparrows, blue tits and chaffinches choose their mates and look for a safe, sheltered spot to build their nests.

The furry catkins of pussy-willow are a sign that spring is coming.

By May, the hedgerow teems with tiny creatures.
There's fresh food for new arrivals. Butterfly and moth eggs hatch into caterpillars which munch bramble leaves. Great tits pick off the caterpillars and feed them to their young.

In summer the hedgerow buzzes with insects.

Look out for the magpie moth in the hawthorn.

Birds feed in the early morning and late afternoon.

When the sun is hottest, at midday, they find shade. Young birds have left the nest and learned to fly. Now they can feed themselves. Linnets find grass seeds, cuckoos catch caterpillars, blackbirds find plenty of worms. Thrushes hammer snails from their shells. And all the birds sing from the top of the hedge.

The hedgehog comes out of hiding after dark, in search of slugs and snails to eat.

A passing grass snake will be a tasty snack!

On a warm afternoon, you can hear many insects. Bees and butterflies feast on pollen and nectar from hedgerow flowers. Crickets and grasshoppers enjoy juicy green leaves.

In summer there are few hours of darkness.

The animals which hunt by night have no time to waste!

Owls start hunting soon after dark. Listen for a tell-tale hoot, and on a clear night you may even see the owl outlined against the sky. It is searching for a field-mouse, vole or shrew. The faintest rustle amongst the leaves brings it swooping silently down, its amber eyes staring. Owls eat the rats and mice which feed on the farmer's crops.

In autumn the hedgerow is laden with food.

Rosehips

Blackberries

Haws (hawthorn berries)

Hazelnuts

Elderberries

Crab-apples

Holly berries

Sloes from the blackthorn

By September the hedgerow fruits are ripe.

The flowers of spring and summer have left behind little clusters of fruit, which have swelled and ripened in the sun. Now comes the time to gather nuts and berries. The birds know which berries are good to eat, but you must be careful! Many berries, like the bright red holly, are poisonous. Others, like the tasty-looking elderberry, need cooking. Ask an adult to help you.

The hedgehog has eaten his fill and settles down to sleep.

Food for all!

Voles and mice hide hazelnuts and crab-apples in hollow trees. Their larders will help them through the winter. Pheasants scratch around for acorns, berries, seeds and snails buried in the undergrowth beside the hedge. The fox creeps along the base of the hedge, keeping an eye out for his next meal – a plump field mouse or a juicy root.

Blackbirds gorge themselves on blackberries and elderberries.

But life in the hedgerow is hard in winter.

Mistletoe sucks sap from trees. It is a parasite*.

People pick sprigs of holly, butcher's broom and mistletoe to decorate their houses for Christmas.

Holly

Butcher's broom

Berries turn soft after the first frost, the last leaves are blown off the trees, and the hedgerow is quiet and stripped for winter.

Many small animals hibernate* until spring.

They have eaten or stored enough food to last them through the winter. Hedgehogs and dormice settle down to sleep among dead leaves. Field mice and bank voles have stored grain in their burrows. Other creatures stay awake through winter. Insects feed on dead leaves. Shrews feed on the insects. Robins, wrens and hedge-sparrows come to the hedge to look for food. If they are lucky they will find insects and worms here even in the coldest weather.

Earthworms help to clean up the hedgerow.

They drag down tiny pieces of leaf to eat in their underground tunnels. In time, the rest of the leaves will rot down into leaf-mould*. This provides a rich, fertile* soil to feed the plants when spring comes and the hedgerow bursts into life once again.

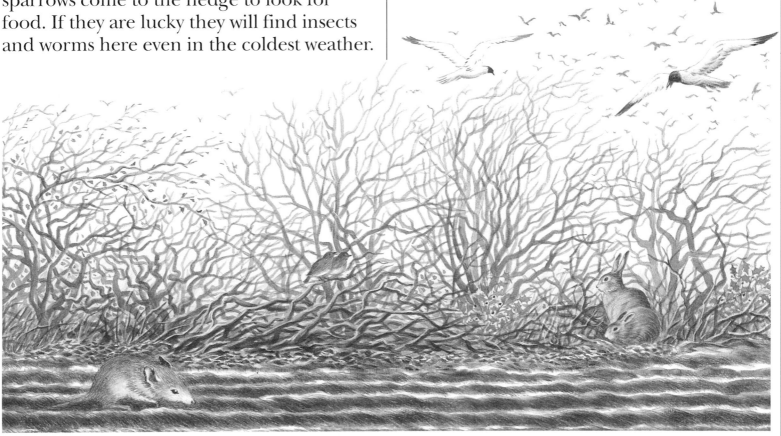

A whole world within the hedgerow!

<u>Every living thing plays an important part in the life of the hedge.</u> Plants and animals rely on one another for food and shelter. The hedgerow is an ecosystem*.

Butterflies and moths lay their eggs in the spring on the leaves the caterpillars will feed on. Blue tits prey* on the caterpillars: they can catch up to 400 a day to feed their young. In turn, blue tits may be prey to weasels and foxes.

Fresh green leaves are attacked by swarms of tiny greenfly, or aphids, which suck their sap. Luckily for the hedgerow, ladybirds find aphids good to eat!

Wild herbs and climbing plants add colour and scent.

Climbing towards the sunlight

Most plants have strong stems and grow upright towards the light, but others need support. They cling to other plants, scrambling up through trees and bushes to reach the sunshine.

Climbing plants hold on in different ways. Goose grass sticks to plants with the tiny hairs on its leaves. White bryony sends out little corkscrew tendrils. Bindweed and most honeysuckles twine themselves round their host plants.

When they reach the top of the hedge, these creepers spill over in a tangled mass of leaves and flowers.

Poppies, wild chicory and cornflowers bloom in summer between hedge and field.

Wild flowers grow along the base of the hedge,

where there is shade and shelter. You may find foxgloves, cowslips, lady's smock, wild mint, vetch, common mallow and ox-eye daisies. If you are very lucky you may even see wild orchids.

When you walk in tall grass, wear long socks or boots to protect your legs from thistles and stinging nettles.

Some of the wild flowers that grow near hedges are now rare. Only pick flowers if you know there are lots more. You can always enjoy them where they grow.

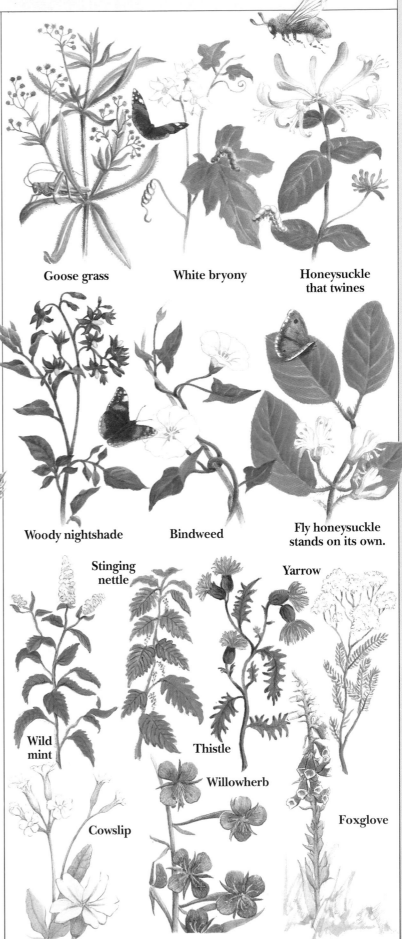

Goose grass

White bryony

Honeysuckle that twines

Woody nightshade

Bindweed

Fly honeysuckle stands on its own.

Stinging nettle

Yarrow

Wild mint

Thistle

Willowherb

Cowslip

Foxglove

Trout   Char   Eel

Spring water and melted snow tumble down the mountains in cold, bubbling torrents. Lower down, the streams flow more slowly and are warmed by the sun. Several join together to become a river. From the source to the mouth of the river, thousands of different plants and animals make this habitat* their home.

Grizzly bears
fish for salmon
in a Canadian river.

Eels hatch in the Sargasso Sea.
After two years drifting with the current, they reach land and move up-river. Ten years later the adult eels go down-river again and back out to sea. They return to the Sargasso Sea to spawn* and die.

Larvae find different materials for their protective casing: grains of sand, twigs, pieces of leaf.

The larvae of mayflies and caddisflies spend up to two years under water.
In fast-flowing streams, these insect larvae encase themselves in little open-ended tubes made of sand, twigs, or leaves. Their fragile body is protected from predators* like the dragonfly and from the rough and tumble of life in the river. Some larvae even anchor themselves to a stone or a shell so they cannot be washed along in the current.

At the first sign of danger, the mayfly larva retreats into its case.

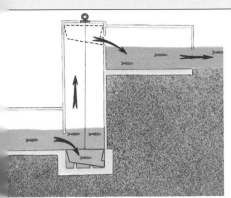

A salmon lift built into a dam. It helps salmon return up-river to spawn*.

Salmon migrate* over huge distances.

Baby salmon, or salmon fry, hatch in rivers in the spring. They stay in the river for their first year. In their second year, when they are about the size of your hand, they begin their long journey down-river towards the sea.

Salmon spend three or four years at sea before returning to their birthplace, up-river. The scent of the home stream guides them back. They swim against the current all the way, covering 30 to 100 kilometres a day. Although many die of exhaustion on the way, many also complete the journey and spawn before they die.

Fish breathe in oxygen under water.

Perch

Water creatures need oxygen like all living things. Oxygen* is in the water which fish suck into their mouths. The oxygen is kept inside the fish's body, while the water is pushed out again through the fish's gills* at the sides of its head.

The crayfish, like the mussel, lives in deep water. Its gills look like soft feathers on its thorax, under the shell.

Herons prey* on fish as well as frogs and small mammals.

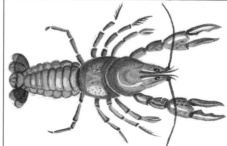

Fresh water crayfish

Water insects, like their cousins in the air above, take in oxygen through tubes called tracheae, making frequent trips to the surface to get more air.

Water spiders make webs among water plants and fill them with air from above the water surface.

Water beetles carry spare air under their wings or among the hairs on their body.

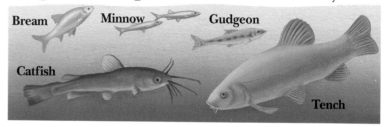

Bream   Minnow   Gudgeon

Catfish

Tench

Tadpoles have an external gill on each side of their neck. As they grow into adult frogs, they develop lungs.

Some freshwater snails have lungs and take oxygen from the water surface or from air bubbles trapped under water. Other snails breathe through gills.

Some fish build nests. This three-spined stickleback digs a little trench on the river bottom and fills it with weed which it sticks together. The female is brought to the nest and swims through it, laying her eggs. The male follows and fertilizes them. He will look after the eggs until they hatch.

Musk-rats and otters build tunnels and lodges.

Musk-rats have several litters of babies every year – up to four families of seven or eight babies each.

Cousins of the beaver

The musk-rat was kept for its fur in North America but later escaped into the wild. In Britain the same thing has happened to the mink, which is a successful predator* of birds, mammals and fish. It competes with the shy otter for food and territory.

Coypus are larger than musk-rats. Their tails are smooth and round, rather than flat like the musk-rat's.

The coypu is a member of the rat family which also escaped from fur farms to naturalize all over Europe. It digs holes in banks which cause flooding in flat areas of land near the sea.

The musk-rat builds his lodge from reed stalks. The entrance is under water.

Otters eat fish, frogs and crustaceans.

Nowadays otters are rarely found in the wild, but they are bred in captivity and then released into the rivers of Britain.

The otter swims gracefully, thanks to its webbed feet. It is also skilled at fishing, and can run fast on land.
The female otter gives birth to her young in a nest in the riverbank.

Kingfishers, gulls, wagtails, ducks, moorhens...

The riverbank bustles with bird life.

If you walk along the riverbank you will see many different signs of life. Perhaps you will spot a swallow dipping for a drink of water, or the blue flash of a kingfisher diving for fish. Look carefully and you may see a moorhen swimming among the reeds.

Gulls sometimes live by rivers and lakes, a long way from the sea.

In spring the water is crowded with baby birds.

The grebe's family is safe in a nest amongst the plants near the water's edge. The young chicks nestle into the feathers on their mother's back.

The grey wagtail lives on the banks of the river, hopping from stone to stone, its tail wagging. It nests in a hole in the riverbank.

Wagtails are found by fast-flowing water. They feed on small insects.

The kingfisher sits motionless on a high branch watching the water below. When it sees a fish, it dives from its perch and stabs the prey* with its long, sharp beak. It may beat the fish on a branch to kill it, and will then swallow it whole, head first. As well as fish, the kingfisher hunts for tadpoles and shellfish.

Imagine how hard the kingfisher must work to feed its young family in spring!

Kingfishers burrow in to the steep riverbank to make their nests. The eggs are laid at the end of a long tunnel.

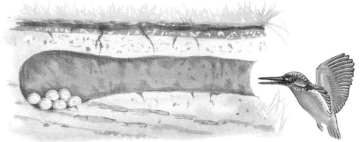

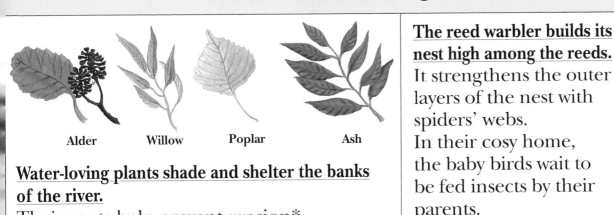

Alder   Willow   Poplar   Ash

Water-loving plants shade and shelter the banks of the river.

Their roots help prevent erosion*.
There are many different species*
of willow. Some grow as trees,
others grow as thick bushes
making safe cover for birds
and small mammals. Willow
branches can be cut and woven
to make baskets and fencing.
The poplar stands tall, giving shade
in the heat of summer. Its leaves
dance and shimmer in the wind.
The fruits of the alder tree look like
fircones. In autumn the seeds fall from
the ripe, brown fruits and float down-river
to new ground.

The moorhen often rears two broods* of chicks each spring.

She makes a nest of twigs and leaves
by the water's edge. When they hatch,
the chicks follow their mother everywhere.
Before these chicks are fully grown, their
mother may hatch a second family.
The older chicks will help to feed
the younger ones.

The reed warbler builds its nest high among the reeds.

It strengthens the outer
layers of the nest with
spiders' webs.
In their cosy home,
the baby birds wait to
be fed insects by their
parents.

Reed warbler

The adult birds'
brown colour gives
them camouflage*
among the reeds as
they come and go
to the nest of chicks.

The moorhen's four long
toes help it walk across soft
mud without sinking in.

A hollow in the ground becomes a pond.

Many secrets hide behind the thick curtain of plants around the pond. In the water, on its surface, around its banks, the pond supports life of many different kinds. A pond, or even a lake, can form wherever rainwater collects. Some places are kinder to water life than others. A small pool dries up in summer, and in a lake with deep, dark water fewer plants will grow.

In the Middle Ages, people dug ponds to breed fish.

Some ponds form naturally.
Rainwater is trapped in hollows and cannot seep away through the soil. Water plants quickly take root in the uneven ground.

Plants find it hard to grow on steep banks.

Other ponds and lakes are man-made.
Some form in the pits left where people have dug up peat or sand. After a few years they look natural.
Gardeners may make ponds to grow water plants or attract water creatures.
Sometimes several ponds are joined together into one big lake – perhaps to make a reservoir or a fish farm. These lakes are regularly dredged* and cleaned.

As the banks of the pond are worn and washed away they become less steep. Plants take root more easily.

Birds, fish and plants make the pond their home.

A deserted sand-pit slowly becomes a pond.

Fewer animals are found in ponds and lakes where boating and fishing are allowed.

Plants quickly colonize* a new pond.

Plant seeds are carried by birds or on the wind. The seedlings* soon take root.

Soon animals and fish begin to breed in the pond.

Humans can frighten the animals away. It may be years before they return.

Plants and animals depend on one another.

Tiny algae and animals thrive in pond water.

These minute plants and creatures are called plankton. Look at a drop of pond water through a strong magnifying glass or a microscope – you'll be able to see the plankton.

Plankton – the beginning of the food chain*

Insect larvae will eat the plankton. Fish and birds will eat the larvae.

In turn, the fish and birds will be food for larger predators*.

The freshwater mussel feeds on microscopic plants, siphoning them between its two shells.

Small shellfish and worms keep the pond bottom clean by eating any pieces of dead plant which drift down there.

Water snails feed on the algae that grow on underwater stems and rocks. Young tadpoles feed on water plants, but as they grow older they eat the remains of dead fish too.

Tadpoles make easy prey* for dragonfly and water beetle larvae, fish and scorpions.

Kingfisher

Frog

Water boatman

Water scorpion

Tadpoles

Carp

Water beetle

Crayfish

Plenty of food for all in the pond

A frog eats thousands of insects, slugs, worms and snails in the course of its life. But it has its own enemies too. Fish, kingfishers and grass snakes all like to eat frogs.

Many insects begin their life in the pond.

The female mosquito lays her eggs in the still water. Adult mosquitoes hatch from the larvae after only a few days. Dragonfly larvae stay in the water for up to two years. From the moment they hatch, winged, adult dragonflies are fierce hunters of insects, tadpoles and even tiny fish.

Grass snakes, toads, newts and frogs live near water too.

Frogs, newts and toads spend much of the year on land. In spring, they look for still water where they can lay their eggs. The female frog lays her eggs in the water from March and the eggs are fertilized by the male. The frogspawn swells to a jelly-like mass in the water. Two or three weeks later, the tadpoles hatch.
Grass snakes hatch on land but make straight for the water.

The European pond tortoise is now very rare and in danger of extinction.

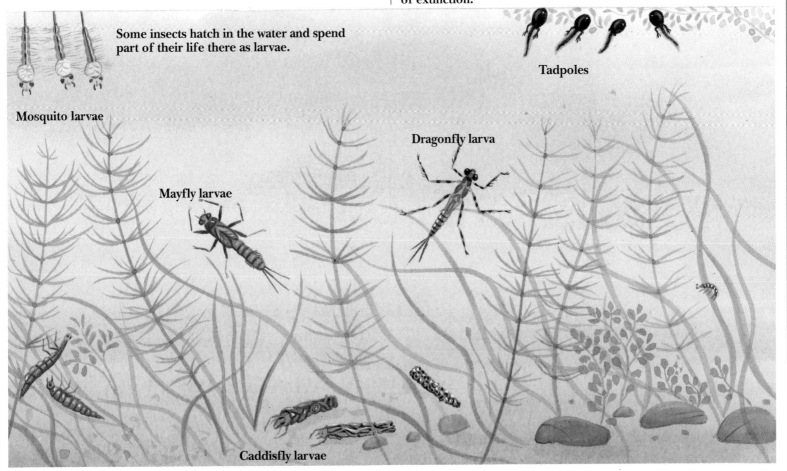

Some insects hatch in the water and spend part of their life there as larvae.

Tadpoles

Mosquito larvae

Dragonfly larva

Mayfly larvae

Caddisfly larvae

Water birds come and go.

The grebe chick's colouring gives it camouflage* from its predators*.

Food and shelter for birds

Birds build their nests among the rushes and reeds at the pond's edge, safe from their enemies. Ducks dabble among the weeds and turn up their tails as they look below water. Grebes dive for small fish, they can stay under water for several minutes. At the first sign of danger, all the birds rise noisily into the air. They will circle in the air and land on the pond when it is safe again.

Mallard ducks are common on the ponds and lakes of Britain. The female is dull brown for camouflage* but the male is more brightly coloured.

Migrating birds stop to break their journey.

Many ducks, geese and swans spend the summer months in the cooler north, in Scandinavia. There they can feed throughout the long, light days.
As autumn approaches they fly south in V formation, in search of warmth. The strongest take turns to lead, finding their way by the Sun and the stars.
They are exhausted after their long journey and need to feed and rest. You may see them on British ponds where they stop to spend the winter.
Whooper and Bewick swans graze with geese beside ponds. Teal, pochard and tufted duck dive for water weeds and insects.
As spring approaches, they will fly north again to nest.

In spring the male and female grebe dance together. The male offers the female some twigs and grass for her nest.

The pond changes with the seasons.

It is summer. The grass snake feeds on frogs, tadpoles and fish, eating them whole.

It is winter. The grass snakes hibernate* together under a stone or in a hole.

In summer the water near the surface of the pond warms up. Pond creatures dive into deeper water to cool themselves.
In hot weather, algae spreads quickly and the water looks quite green. Meadowsweet and buttercups flower around the pond.

In winter the pond may be covered with ice. Fish take refuge in deep water, sheltered from the frost. Insect larvae and newts lie buried in the mud. Ducks and other birds slither across the ice in search of water. Willow twigs rattle in the winter wind.

An underwater forest!

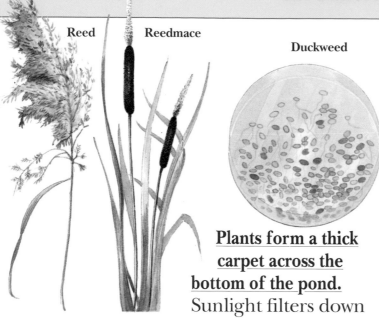

Reed Reedmace

Duckweed

Sundew plants have no green leaves. Instead the leaves are covered with sticky traps which catch and dissolve small insects like flies.

Plants form a thick carpet across the bottom of the pond.

Sunlight filters down to them through the still, shallow water. Water plants supply the pond creatures with all they need to live: oxygen*, shelter and food. Plant-eating animals nibble away at the vegetation and stop the pond from becoming overgrown.

The duckweed shown here is one of the smallest flowering plants. It is the size of rice grains, but it can reproduce fast in sunshine and soon spreads across the pond. It is a floating plant: its roots take their food from water.

Water-lily roots are anchored to the pond bottom.

The flowers and leaves have long stems so that they float on the surface of the water.

In summer, reeds grow high around the pond.

By the end of the year, their thick roots and the remains of their great stems can fill a shallow pond. They rot down through the winter.

Rotting plants may finally clog the pond – it will become a muddy bog. Insects will hatch from eggs in the mud. Insect-eating plants and other species* which can colonize* the mud will appear. Soon other land plants take root and the wetland* community will have disappeared.

Ponds and lakes need our protection.

Pollution* from factories and sewage-works kills many pond animals and water plants. The food chain is easily broken.

Wildlife reserves are created from reservoirs, flooded quarries and fields, and man-made holes. This helps to make up for the disappearing natural habitats* like ponds and wetlands. In some reserves there are planned walks you can follow. You will learn more about how birds and animals live in the wild. You will learn to identify different species* too. In reserves, plants and wild animals come first and we learn to observe them without disturbing them.

Nowadays many ponds are dying.

The lives of plants and animals living there are endangered. Ponds used to help drain the fields, and farm animals drank from them. But now farmers have new drainage systems and can pipe water to their animals, so they don't need ponds. Sometimes farmers drain ponds and wetlands* to make fields larger, but this can upset the balance of nature and crops may grow poorly.

The osprey feeds on fish from ponds and lakes. It is now an endangered species*.

Ponds and lakes are drained to make extra land for building. Near towns, ponds, lakes and waterways are cleaned up for bathing and the plants on the banks are cut back. The animals that lived there move away or die.

We can protect natural habitats* so that birds and animals can live there without being disturbed.

High up in the mountains...

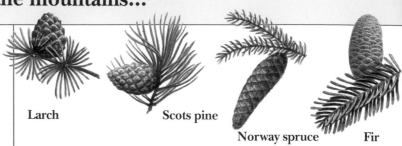

Larch Scots pine

Norway spruce Fir

The higher you climb in the mountains, the colder it gets. The temperature drops about one degree centigrade for every 200 metres you rise. Different plants grow at different levels. Deciduous* trees are found in the valleys and conifers on the higher slopes. Right at the top of the mountain, where the wind blows icy cold, no trees grow at all. A few small plants manage to survive the harsh winters to blossom in a brightly coloured carpet in spring.

Which trees grow in the mountains?

Conifers, mainly. Their needles are resistant to drought and frost. Many conifers are evergreen: their needles don't fall in winter. Larches need a lot of sunlight – you find them above the clouds. Fir trees like rain and mist. They grow on north-facing slopes where less light falls. Did you know the spruce is a Christmas tree? It likes sunshine and shade. Scot's pine grows anywhere, as long as it's not too hot. Squirrels love to eat its tiny cones.

Conifers are well suited to the harsh conditions in the mountains. They can withstand severe cold and the weight of the snow on their branches.

Sweet chestnut

Green alder

Oak

Sycamore

Birch

Lime

The trees protect the mountain soil.

If the slopes are cleared of trees, rainwater and melting snow fall directly onto the ground. Muddy streams form and drag the fertile top soil down to the valley causing landslides and flooding.

Grizzly bears live in the conifer forests of Alaska, Canada and parts of Siberia.

In summer the mountains come to life.

On the lower slopes oak, chestnut and beech trees stand amongst the conifers. Higher up, in the fir forest, it may seem bleak, it is so dark and humid. But in clearings and along the paths, you'll find wild strawberries and bilberry bushes laden with delicious fruit.

People keep cows, sheep and goats which they take out to pasture on the high meadows in summer. As autumn approaches the animals are sheltered in stables or taken down to the lower valleys where it never gets quite as cold. Nowadays, few families are left in the villages. There is little work to be found and many of the young people have moved to the cities. But in the summer months, the wild flowers, the fresh air and the peace attract holidaymakers escaping the city.

In summer the meadows burst into colour.

Sedum can hold water in its leaves.

In the mountains alpenrose, a dwarf rhododendron, grows no higher than your knee.

Mountain pansies are related to the violets of temperate woodlands.

In mountain meadows thistles grow close to the ground.

Above the tree line it is cold and windy.

If you look at a range of mountains you notice that no trees grow above a certain altitude. Over about 2,500 metres weather conditions are too harsh for trees. Here there are meadows of shrubs, small plants and grasses. Many find shelter in cracks between the rocks, their deep roots anchoring them in place. Dwarf varieties of common plants found in the valleys below also grow well.

Many mountain plants are protected.

You mustn't pick or damage them. Don't gather flowers on your walks. They soon droop, and it is sad to see a withered bunch of flowers discarded by the side of the path. Enjoy the flowers where they grow and leave them for others to see. Remember, plants are the foundation of all food chains*. In the mountains they have to struggle to survive – don't make it more difficult for them!

Conditions are hard at high altitude.

Saxifrage

Gentian

Columbine

Arnica

Alpine plants grow on high peaks.

All year round they are battered by freezing winds, ice and snow. That's why they grow small and gnarled. Their leaves are leathery to stop the wind drying them up and the plant looks like a cushion. During winter everything is covered with a thick blanket of snow which stops the ground from freezing. When spring comes and the snow melts, the ground swells with water. The plants bloom, covering the mountain in bright colours. These alpine plants have become favourites for gardens too.

Edelweiss grows at altitudes between 1,700 and 3,400 metres.

Its flowers, which bloom in summer, have a lovely downy look. But so many people have picked it that the plant has become quite rare.

The leaves of the edelweiss are covered with a fine down which protects the plant from the cold.

Many mountain plants have small leaves and vivid colours

St John's wort hides in cracks between the rocks away from the howling wind.

Bilberries can be used to make delicious jam.

Many different sorts of animals...

The chamois is a wild goat that lives on steep mountains. Before it is 6 months old the mother has taught the young chamois to leap from crag to crag.

Chamois, ibex and wild sheep live on high mountain slopes. Their hard, sharp hooves grip the rocks like pincers, helping them to climb without slipping.

Chamois can leap up to eight metres.

When danger threatens they whistle to alert the whole herd. In summer these sure-footed creatures climb as high as the glaciers, feeding on herbs and flowers in the meadows. In winter they come down to the conifer forests, to shelter among the trees and eat young shoots.

Ibex eat bushes and grasses.

Life is hard in winter.

Snow covers the grass and it is difficult to find food. Some animals like marmots hibernate*. In autumn they feast on grasses, grains and fruit, before curling up in their burrows for a long winter sleep. Their breathing slows down and their body temperature falls.

Marmots sleep the whole winter away.

They wake up in spring when it begins to get warm. Animals that stay outdoors may change the colour of their coat. In the winter landscape they can move about unseen, whether they are hunting or being hunted.

Arctic hares turn white in winter with only a small tip of their tail remaining black.

Ermines are stoats which have changed their summer brown coat to white.

A ptarmigan's summer (above) and winter (below) feathers. At night it digs out a little shelter for itself in the snow.

The mouflon is a wild mountain sheep.

These herbivores* will eat any plant, gorging on the young shoots, the flowers, or even the whole bush. In summer the young live with their mother, while the males form their own group. Their huge, curled horns weigh up to 6 kilos. Mouflons came originally from Corsica and Sardinia but are now found all over Europe.

The Apollo butterfly is a protected species*. As a caterpillar it is black with red and blue dots. It feeds on stonecrop.

The Spanish moon moth flies both day and night. It lives in pine forests.

In summer the meadows swarm with insects.

Butterflies and grasshoppers take advantage of the short warm season to feed and mate. Some species* of butterflies, like many of the plants here, are protected. But butterfly catchers still look for the prettiest species to pin up in display cases. As they are threatened also by pollution*, there is a serious risk that butterflies will disappear altogether.

In winter the wild sheep's fur is rough and brownish black.

Grizzly bears like to be alone.

These two cubs were born in winter. They play by their den while their mother goes hunting.

Spring is here!

The mother bear hasn't eaten since autumn and has used up most of the body fat she had stored. She must go out in search of food for herself and her cubs.

But mother bear is watchful: other bears and wolves can kill young cubs.

A cosy den to sleep away the winter

As soon as the weather turns cold, a grizzly will dig itself a hole underneath a rock or a fallen tree and line the floor with a thick layer of dry grass. It settles in as soon as the first snow falls – that way no tracks will lead to its hide-out, where it will sleep through till spring.

Bears will eat almost anything!

They like plants, berries and nuts, insect grubs and fish, as well as young animals. Sometimes they'll even attack a ewe or deer. Weighing up to 200 kilos, they are powerful predators*.
But grizzly bears are generally peaceful. They usually live alone, avoiding other animals, especially people. There are not many places they can live quietly now. They are protected, but there are only a few left, hidden away in wild mountain ranges.

The mother teaches the cubs what to eat. She has to dig up roots for them and pick berries. She will look after the cubs for 18 months before they start life on their own.

Birds must find food thoughout the winter.

Speckled nutcracker

Dipper

Ring ouzel

Siskin   Rock pipit   Coaltit

Birds living in the mountains have a thick layer of fat under their feathers.

This helps keep their body temperature at 41 degrees centigrade.
Birds like the rock pipit, which lives up by the highest peaks in summer, have to come down to the forest in winter to find food.
On freezing winter nights, coaltits huddle together in their holes to keep warm.

Nutcrackers eat hazel nuts and pine kernels.

In summer they gather as much food as they can for the winter. Each bird can carry up to 60 seeds at a time thanks to a special pocket under its tongue. They hide their store at the base of a tree so that they will have food throughout the cold months.

The ouzel eats insects and small fish from mountain streams. Its young know how to swim even before they can fly.

The Black grouse lives in quiet forests. It is twice as large as a chicken, and its claws are arranged in a fan shape to help it walk on thick snow.

Eagles perch their nests on top of the highest craggy peaks.

An eagle spots its prey* from high up and circles before plunging down for the kill. Eagles hunt marmots, hares and even young chamois.

47

On the seashore, the rhythm of the tides

Have you been to the seaside? It's the place where three different environments come together: the sea, the land and the air.

Some shores have cliffs and are rocky, some are sandy, others are muddy.

The sea rises and falls twice a day: these are tides. Plants and animals which live along the shore survive in conditions which change as the tide goes in and out. At high tide, these plants and creatures may be drenched in salty water, at low tide they may dry out in the heat of the sun.

The sea throws up all sorts of things onto the beach: seaweed, shells, feathers. They collect in a wavy line we call the high water mark. Flies and sandhoppers feed on rotting seaweed.

Along flat, open coastlines where there is little shelter, the wind blows the sand into dunes. Plants growing on dunes have to live in dry, salty conditions.

Sea purslane and golden samphire grow on the slopes of salt-marshes.

Marram grass helps to stabilize* the sand, and sea-holly has roots which go down 3 metres. Creeping sea-bindweed can cling on even in the strongest winds. Amongst the dunes you may also find carpets of sea-rocket and scurvy grass.

If the plants die, the dunes become unstable and the sand is blown away on the wind.

The common shore crab likes the muddy sea-bed, but you may also see one on the sand or rocks. If it senses danger, it will rear up, stretch out its claws and clack them together. Or it may just burrow into the sand.

Flowers you might see on a beach in France

Marestail grass

Sea-holly

Sea-rocket

Sea-spurge

Sea-bindweed

Sea-aster

Immortelle flower

Thousands of creatures lie hidden in the sand.

At low tide, lugworms leave coils of sand from their diggings.

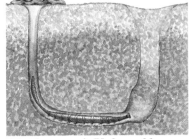

The lugworm's U-shaped burrow

Transparent sand-eels burrow into sandbanks.

If you walk over the wet sand in bare feet, watch out for the sharp spines of the weever fish. They are poisonous.

The sand on a beach is made up of countless tiny grains.

Many are pieces of a mineral called quartz, but there are fragments of seashells as well.

The beach may look deserted at low tide,

but there are animals living in the warm, damp sand and mud. The lugworm swallows sand as it makes its tunnel, digesting any food and casting the rest in coils on the surface.

The razor-shell can bury itself in the sand in less than a minute. It uses its single foot as an anchor and pulls itself down.

Starfish, shrimps and crabs hide in the sand until high tide. Then they come out in search of food.

Cockles, clams and razor-shells are bi-valves. They have two shells to protect their soft body. They are members of the mollusc family. They dig into the sand, pushing out a strong foot to hold on as they pull themselves down. At high tide they put up two siphons* to the surface. One sucks in sea water containing food, waste is pushed out through the other.

The razor-shell puts out its siphons* to feed.

The cockle anchors itself in the sand with its strong foot.

At high tide, the cockle feeds from the sea water.

Crustaceans and seaweed cling to the rocks.

At low tide, the sea anemone draws in its tentacles and closes up so that it does not dry out.

On a rocky shore plants and animals fight for their life.

They have to withstand strong winds and salt spray. The limpet has a foot which acts as a sucker, allowing the animal to glide over the rocks and graze on seaweed. Acorn barnacles, on the other hand, stay in one spot.

Mussels attach themselves to rocks with byssus, hair-like strands produced from a gland in their foot. When they move, they fix new threads onto the rock from one side and break the old ones.

What is seaweed?

It is an aquatic* plant which does not have separate flowers, leaves or roots. Instead it is made up of a thallus – a single piece of plant tissue.

Some seaweeds drift, others fix themselves to rocks and shells with a holdfast. Several kinds are edible. Their soft fronds waft in the water. Some seaweeds have slimey fronds so they don't dry out at low-tide. Delicate species* have adapted* to life in rock pools, where the water is calmer and conditions are not so changeable.

Orange shield lichen	Black tar lichen	Flat wrack	Periwinkle
Edible winkle	Chiton shell	Limpet	Topshell
Bladder wrack	Acorn barnacle	Mussels covered with barnacles	Ormer

Himanthalia elongata, or thongweed

Sugar kelp

Fucus serratus, or serrated wrack

Sea lettuce

Bladder wrack

Carragheen

Sea-birds shelter among the cliffs.

Sea-birds lay their eggs on rocky ledges.
In spring, the cliff face rings with the cries of the adult birds and the cheeping of their hungry chicks. The kittiwake builds a strong and stable nest with mud, seaweed, grass and droppings. The puffin uses its bill to hollow out a burrow for its eggs. Guillemots lay a single egg which is pear-shaped to stop it rolling off the ledge. Like razorbills, they are expert at fishing under water, and only come to land to nest and raise their chicks.

Puffin

Kittiwake

The petrel glides just above the surface of the waves.

Cormorant

Razorbill

Gannet

Guillemot

Rock pools are left as the tide goes out.

What can you see when you look into a rock pool?

Water caught among the rocks warms up in the sun. Rock pools make the perfect home for seaweed, molluscs, small fish, crabs and shrimps.

You might see a sea-urchin creeping slowly across the bottom of the pool, or a star-fish using its arms to open a shell.

Watch the crab scuttle sideways

and hide under seaweed. See how the hermit crab borrows the shell of another animal to protect its soft body!

Sea-urchin

What can the shrimp find to eat?

A little bit of everything: tiny creatures, algae, pieces of dead fish...

The rising tide will bring fresh food for all in the rock pool.

Crab

Sea-urchin

Shrimp

Star-fish

Hermit crab

Brightly coloured fish in warmer seas

All around the Mediterranean coast

are meadows of Neptune grass which animals use as larders and shelters. The sea-hare (1) lays its eggs in long strands which fishermen call sea spaghetti. The male sea-horse (2) looks after its eggs in a pouch on its abdomen. Bass (3) and red mullet (4) scour the water in search of food. Some fish can hurt you. Look out for the sting-ray (5), its tail is armed with sharp spines. The tentacles of the jelly-fish (6) can sting you even after it is dead.

Sponge

Tropical coasts fringed with coral reefs

Coral forms from animals called polyps, whose bodies are like tiny sacs. Their skeletons pile on top of each other, over many years, eventually making a hard limestone mass. Exotic fish live among the coral: butterfly fish, lion fish, angel fish. The fierce-looking lion fish uses its huge fins as a net to trap its prey.

Butterfly fish

Lion fish

Angel fish

Sea-pen

The sea: a source of great wealth

People have always dived for sponges, corals and pearls.

Divers without air tanks can go down to 6 metres and stay under water for 2 or 3 minutes before coming up for air.

Diving for the riches of the sea

For thousands of years, men have dived and fished for the sea's treasures.
Now scientists have explored the oceans and have discovered new treasures: salt, minerals*, gas and oil very deep below the surface.

Huge platforms are built to pump oil from the bottom of the sea. They have to be strong enough to withstand the roughest storms.

Oil and metals under the sea.

There are vast reserves of oil under the sea floor and every metal in the world can be found dissolved in sea water, even gold.
So far we have only drilled for a small amount of oil and the metals are difficult to extract. Only magnesium and bromine can be separated and used.

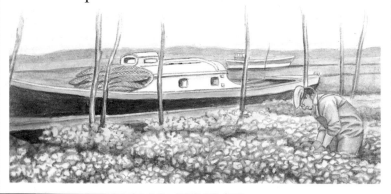

Modern trawlers catch thousands of fish.

The catch is processed on board and delivered to the port already frozen and boxed. This way of fishing is efficient but fish numbers are dropping, particularly near polluted* coasts. Over-fishing has become a serious problem, and in some areas there aren't enough adult fish left to breed. Drag nets collect not only the fish we want but other animals like porpoises in the North Sea. Dolphins get tangled in tuna nets and die in great numbers. Unwanted, they are thrown back into the sea.

Nowadays fish and shellfish are farmed.

Scientists and farmers are learning more about how each type of fish lives so they can be reared in large numbers. In the future you may eat only farmed fish and shellfish. Seaweed is farmed too.

Pearls form inside some oyster shells.

It is rich in minerals*, especially iodine, and very good for you. Welsh laver bread, made from a purple seaweed, is a great delicacy. Agar can be extracted from seaweed to make jelly and for use in cosmetics.

In the bay, oyster farmers grow young oysters on sheets covered with sand.

The oceans play an important part in our planet's life. Scientists believe that all life began in the seas some 3,000 million years ago. Today the oceans contain much food needed by plants and animals and many gases, like oxygen*, vital to life on Earth.

We must protect our seas! If an oil tanker is shipwrecked and spills its load into the sea, the oil smothers and kills the creatures that live in the water and along the coast. We've seen a number of these accidents in the last few years and we still don't know the full extent of the damage.

People sometimes treat the sea as a rubbish bin, tossing refuse into it from boats and at the seaside. But when we poison the sea, we poison everything that lives in it.

1. Plankton
2. Sardines
3. Portuguese man-o'-war
4. Manta ray
5. Killer whale
6. Dolphin
7. Mackerel
8. Tuna
9. Octopus
10. Baleen whale
11. Cod
12. Shark
13. Barracuda
14. Sperm whale
15. Giant squid
16. Squid
17. Hatchet fish
18. Gulper eel
19. Viperfish
20. Angler fish
21. Lantern fish
22. Tripod fish
23. Brittlestar
24. Sea anemone

lar regions
er?
s.
ong,
warmth.
iperature
ees
red with
m rains,
nd and
e animals

Emperor penguins live in Antarctica. This seal is sliding across the ice on its belly, like a toboggan!

Seals only spend part of their lives on land or on ice-floes.

In winter they make holes in the ice to breathe through when they're fishing in the water below. Polar bears lie in wait and try to catch them when they poke their noses out.

The cold doesn't worry polar bears. Their bodies are covered with a thick layer of fat under their fur coat. Their massive size helps maintain their body warmth. But they do need a lot to eat: up to 100 kilos of fish at one meal!

In summer whales feed on the huge amounts of krill* in the polar waters.

Birds breed there and feed on the krill, too. Penguins live at the South Pole in colonies of up to 10,000 individuals. They migrate to warmer waters to breed.

The walrus has large tusks which it uses to dig for shellfish on the sea bottom, and to haul itself onto ice-floes.

Some Lapps in Scandinavia still follow the reindeer herds and use them to pull their sledges and carry their belongings.

Around the edge of the Arctic ice-cap, the ground of the tundra is frozen solid.

Only lichen and a few birch trees grow here. This is the world of the reindeer. Its fur, made of hollow hairs filled with air, gives it superb insulation against the cold. Its big hooves hardly sink into the snow at all.

Snowy owls look like fluffy balls of white feathers. They feed on lemmings which they hunt by day.

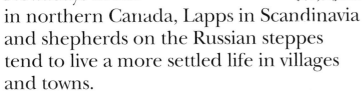

Nomadic peoples used to roam these frozen territories. Nowadays Inuits in northern Canada, Lapps in Scandinavia and shepherds on the Russian steppes tend to live a more settled life in villages and towns.

Reindeer live in herds.

Known as caribou in Canada, they feed on young grasses in the open plains of the north. In autumn they gather in their thousands and begin the journey south to warmer climates. Wolves follow, waiting for the older and weaker animals to collapse.

Reindeer that are left behind risk dying in a snow storm.

When the snow melts the ground becomes a swamp. Thousand of midges and other insects hatch, providing food for the birds that fly north to rear their young.
By July the tundra is covered with flowers.

The Amazon rainforest, rich in fabulous plants...

It is incredibly hot in the jungle and there are sudden violent storms which leave the air more humid than before. There are no seasons and the climate is the same all year round. Even the length of day and night is always the same. This provides a very stable environment for plants and animals. It is perfect for plant growth and means plants can flower, produce fruit or seeds and lose their leaves at any time of the year. The rainforest is the richest ecosystem* on our planet.

Many of the trees grow up to 60 metres high. But the soil is poor and tree roots don't go deep. Some trees have extra roots coming down from their branches, others grow solid buttresses at the base of their trunk. Climbers and creepers hang down like thick ropes, and mosses and lichens grow directly on the tree trunks.

Constant thunderstorms lead to frequent flooding. The flat Amazon basin lies only 6 metres above sea level: it doesn't take long for the water level to rise.

1. Boa constrictor	5. Parrot	9. Morpho butterfly
2. Ring-tailed lemur	6. Toucan	10. Humming bird
3. Armadillo	7. Tapir	11. Ants
4. Tree frog	8. Sloth	

The rainforest is an ecosystem* with an enormous variety of plants and animals. There are monkeys of all kinds and slow-moving sloths that hang upside down by their claws. Anteaters and wild cats prowl the forest floor. Brightly coloured birds flit through the air: toucans, macaws and parrots are a common sight. There are thousands of insects, including enormous butterflies of every imaginable colour. Here you find many more plants and animals than in a temperate forest, but there may only be a few individuals of each species*. Some species only exist in one small part of the forest. When this is cut down they become extinct. **Between 12 and 20 hectares of forest disappear every minute of the day.** The timber* is mainly used to make furniture. The land is used for farming, but it is not very fertile* and after a few years it is useless. But it is too late for the lost parts of the forest. They won't grow again!

The Sahara desert...

The Sahara desert is the largest in the world. It hardly ever rains here and people and animals have to survive much of the time with little water. Creatures hide under stones or in their dens during the day, to avoid being burnt by the sun. Only a few species* of plants manage to withstand this heat.

Here and there green islands appear in the desert. These are oases, where a natural spring rises to the surface. Fringed with palm, date and fig trees, they offer travellers shade and shelter.

This water is a mirage – as you approach it vanishes.

Many desert creatures are sand-coloured for camouflage*.

Jerboas bound along like tiny kangaroos, balancing on their long tufted tails.

The fennec fox only comes out at night. Its huge ears help it to hear its prey* from a great distance. During the day it shelters in its den, dug out under the sand, out of the sun's heat. Its short, sand-coloured fur makes it almost invisible in the desert.

Some of the animals are very dangerous.

A scorpion's tail contains a poison which is injected into anyone unlucky enough to tread on it.

Lizards live amongst the stones. When they are attacked, they defend themselves with their long tail.

Many of the animals sleep through the long periods of drought. This is an efficient way of saving water and food.

Lizard

Cheetah

Jerboa

Scorpion

Fennec fox

A sidewinder slips easily over the soft sand of the dunes leaving its mysterious tracks.

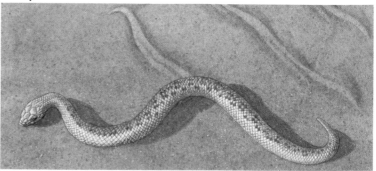

...and its hidden life

The skink doesn't bother to build a nest. It just buries itself in the sand to cool down.

After the rains, colocynths or bitter melons grow in just a few days. They are an important source of water for desert animals.

The Tuareg nomads who travel across the Sahara desert wear loose clothes to protect themselves from sun, wind and sand. Their beast of burden and transport is the camel, the king of the desert. Camels never get lost and can go for a week without water before suffering any ill effects. When they do drink, they can take in over 60 litres at one time. Their hump is a food store and shields their back from the sun.

<u>Desert plants have adapted* to life without rain.</u>
Many will pass much of their lives as seeds, or underground as bulbs or stems. Cacti, for example, are able to live up to a year without rain. They half bury themselves in the sand for protection from the sun's scorching rays. Their stems can expand to store water and then shrink as they dry out. When it finally rains, all the plants flower at once creating an amazing spectacle.

The savanna has a short rainy season.

Between the desert and the rainforest, in a tropical climate, lies the savanna. It is a huge, grassy plain with a few scattered trees.

In the rainy season the grass is fresh and tender.
Herds of migrating* antelopes and zebras come out to feed. Giraffes and elephants come too, but they prefer to eat leaves from the trees. Some of the trees are thorny, but the giraffe's long thin tongue helps it to pluck the young shoots delicately from the stems without pricking itself. Lions can smell a stray or sick zebra from a distance and hunt it down to feed their young.

In the dry season
the trees lose their leaves and the carpet of grasses may be destroyed by sudden fires. The herbivores* will have to travel long distances now to find food and water. But if it rains, tender new shoots appear and the herds of animals return to graze once more.

Games and activities, intriguing facts, a quiz, a glossary, followed by the index

■ Did you know?

The first forests

on Earth developed in the carboniferous era 360 to 286 million years ago. The climate of Europe and North America was warm then, almost tropical. The trees grew very tall and were quite different from trees we know today. In the triassic period (245-208 million years ago) trees similar to our conifers developed, some of which have relatives alive today.

Sap travels from the roots to the branches and takes food right to the tips of the leaves.

Trees don't walk about, trees don't talk, but they are alive.

Just as we do, trees need food and water to live. They draw their food up from the soil. Sap carries goodness from the roots to every twig and leaf. By a process called photosynthesis, trees use the sunlight which shines on their green leaves to make energy. Like all green plants, trees take in carbon dioxide and give off oxygen. We need oxygen in the air we breathe.

What is this fluffy ball?

It is called a rose gall. It grows on dog roses which have been bitten by a black wasp called a gall wasp.

Inside it, in tiny cells, live the larvae – the young of the gall wasp. In spring they grow into adults and come out of their shelter.

Oak apples or oak galls can be seen hanging from oak leaves. They are the home of a tiny maggot which lives on the tree.

Who eats whom?

In nature, each animal has to eat to survive, but each may also be prey to a larger animal.

In the woods the fox eats a weasel (carnivore) who has eaten a field mouse (herbivore) who feeds on grains and tender young shoots.

But who eats the fox?

There are few wolves or lynxes left to attack it. Nowadays foxes usually die of disease or are hunted by humans. Their corpses feed ravens and ants which eat carrion – dead and rotting meat.

The never-ending food chain

One fox alone can eat up to 10,000 rodents a year. So what would happen if there were no more foxes? The field mice would increase in numbers and would end up eating whole fields of corn. The balance of nature would be upset.

Cornflower

■ Did you know?

Plants cure illness.

Our ancestors didn't have medicines like we do, but they used plants to cure their ailments. Many modern medicines are still made from plants.

Mint and camomile are good for the digestion. Poppy petals calm a cough and dock leaves soothe nettle stings.

Poppy

Why do nettles sting?

The tiny hairs that cover the stems and leaves are hollow and full of liquid. They snap off when you touch them letting the stinging liquid drip out onto your skin. True nettles have tiny flowers and always sting. Dead nettles look like stinging nettles, but they don't sting and have more visible flowers.

Yellow dead nettle

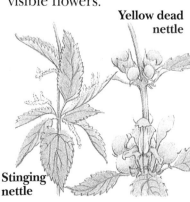

Stinging nettle

Lichens can't survive pollution.

These crust-like plants cling to the surface of bark and rock. They will grow where no other plants can, yet they can't survive in towns or near a factory.

Have you ever seen a fairy ring?

People used to believe circles of mushrooms sprung up where fairies danced. In fact the mushrooms grow from fine underground threads which radiate outwards to form a ring.

■ Can you name these barks?

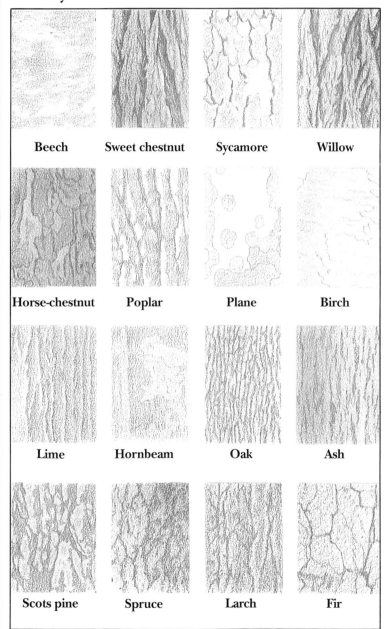

Beech	**Sweet chestnut**	**Sycamore**	**Willow**
Horse-chestnut	**Poplar**	**Plane**	**Birch**
Lime	**Hornbeam**	**Oak**	**Ash**
Scots pine	**Spruce**	**Larch**	**Fir**

Trees such as pines or firs have needle-like leaves

which are lost a few at a time all through the year. They are called conifers. The cones hold their seeds.

Hungry plants

Carnivorous plants live in poor soils which don't provide them with much food. To survive these harsh conditions they catch insects as extra snacks.

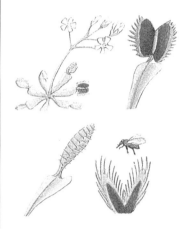

When an insect lands on this Venus fly trap it triggers the spring-trap mechanism. The leaves snap shut and the insect is caught inside. The bowls of the Pitcher plant are full of water. Insects are attracted by the promise of nectar, fall in to the water and drown.

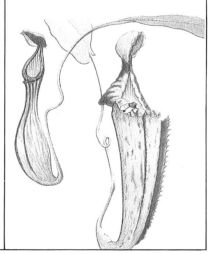

■ Did you know?

Each bird has a beak to suit its food.

Crossbill

Swallow

Thrush

Barn owl

Curlew

Kingfisher

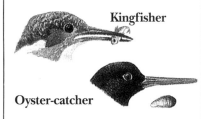
Oyster-catcher

Wasps make paper nests.

They scrape tiny shreds from the bark of trees and mix this up with their saliva. Then they stretch it into thin strips with which to build the cells and the outer shell of the nest. By the end of the summer the nest, which looks like a balloon, may hold up to 25,000 wasps.

Wasp's nest

■ True or false?

Check your answers at the bottom of the next page.

1 You can find out a ladybird's age by counting its spots.

2. Foxes eat fruit such as cherries, plums and grapes.

3. In Canada, some Native Americans make canoes from the bark of birch trees.

4. Cuckoos don't build their own nests.

5. Squirrels build nests in the trees from twigs and moss.

6. Trees sweat in hot weather.

■ Match the flowers and fruits to the tree.

All trees have flowers and fruit.
The flowers aren't always pretty or brightly coloured. Part of each flower turns into a fruit which contains the seeds from which other trees will grow.

These leaves, flowers and fruits belong to some common trees. Can you recognize them?

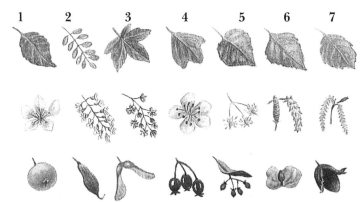

1. Apple tree 2. False acacia 3. Sycamore 4. Hawthorn 5. Lime
6. Birch 7. Hazel 8. Sweet chestnut 9. Hornbeam 10. Beech
11. Ash 12. Spruce 13. Fir 14. Willow

Each bird has its own nest.

Swallow's nest made of mud and saliva

Woodpecker's hole

Petrels lay their eggs in a crack in the cliff.

Weaver bird's hanging nest

There are as many kinds of birds' nests as there are different kinds of birds. Some birds don't bother to build a nest at all; they lay their eggs straight onto the ground. Some use an old nest or lay their eggs in a hollow tree-trunk. Some birds have nests high up in a tree, perched on a branch, some tuck them deep inside a bush...

Shelducks may nest in an old rabbit burrow.

Forest peoples

The Yanomami live in the Amazon rainforest, in leaf-thatched huts. They live in harmony with their environment and take no more from the forest than they need or than it can give.

Living in the Sahara

Vast pebbly plains, dunes of red or white sand stretching as far as the eye can see... this is the Sahara. The Tuareg who live here eat lots of salt because they lose so much of it from their bodies by sweating. Finding water is everyone's main priority and the women sometimes have to walk several kilometres to fill their goatskins at the well.

■ True or false?

7. Some trees have flowers called catkins.

8. If you find a bird's nest in October, you may pick it up and keep it.

9. Doe rabbits make cosy nests right at the bottom of the warren and line them with fur from their own stomachs.

10. The weeping willow grows in forests.

11. Ivy feeds off other trees' sap.

12. Elephants are afraid of mice.

Many millipedes, spiders and other insects live in caves and seldom see the light of day.
They are blind and their bodies are white. Caves may be crisscrossed by underground streams where shrimps and molluscs swim.

1. No. The number of spots will tell you what type of ladybird it is. 2. Yes. 3. Yes. Once the strips of bark are sewn together they form a waterproof shell. 4. No they don't. They lay their eggs in other bird's nests and leave the adoptive parents to care for the chicks when they are born. 5. Yes. They often make more than one nest. 6. Yes. That's what makes the forest cool. 7. Yes. Catkins are tiny flowers without petals which grow on willows, some oaks etc. 8. Yes. Most birds make a new nest every year. 9. Yes. 10. No. Weeping willows don't exist in the wild. 11. No. It grows up tree trunks but has its own roots. 12. Yes.

■ **Learn to love nature and care for it.**

Hiking in the mountains, exploring parks and woods, you learn to enjoy nature and respect it.

Roe deer prints

Dog and fox prints

You'll need good walking boots which support your ankles. Wear dull colours for camouflage and take a warm coat. A pair of binoculars is useful and a notebook to make notes about what you see. Look out for paw and hoof prints, animal dung, bird pellets, the remains of a meal (gnawed pine kernels or nuts) and learn what sort of burrows and nests different animals make. But never disturb a nest or burrow!

Birdwatching
Try to approach the bird downwind (with the wind blowing in your face) so any sound will not carry so easily. Put up a screen of branches so you can move about without frightening the birds. If there is no cover, crawl closer on your elbows and feet. Never make quick movements. You may find a ready-made hide like the one above.

Making a nesting box
Widen the hole in the bottom of a flower pot by tapping it lightly with a hammer. Attach it to a wall sheltered from the wind and from direct sunlight. A great tit may come and nest in it. The birdbox below takes time to make, but you can buy one from a pet shop or garden centre.

In winter mix cooked potatoes and oatmeal with some melted fat and leave it to harden. If you put the mixture outside, tits and finches will come and feed. You can buy specially prepared net bags filled with nuts and hang them outside. Birds will come and feed from them and you'll be able to watch them! Don't put out nuts in the breeding season as chicks may choke on them.

■ Learn to love nature and care for it.

Make a shrimping net.

Find an old potato bag and tie it firmly to a forked stick. You can find all sorts of things in rock pools: shrimps, crabs, molluscs. When you've looked at your catch, return all the creatures to the rock pool.

Scoop up some pond water in a jam jar.

If you cannot visit a pond, collect some water from a puddle or even from a vase of dead flowers. Remember never to go near deep water without an adult.

Look at a drop of water through a microscope or a strong magnifying glass. You will see all sorts of algae, crustaceans and minute transparent creatures.

On the seashore, when the tide is out, you will find all kinds of things to look at.

Slip on your boots or your rubber shoes and take a basket with you. You can collect shells or pebbles of every colour and pattern, polished smooth by the sea. There will be hundreds of them in the sand. But remember, never collect shells with animals living in them – only pick up empty shells.

If you take crabs out of rock pools, always put them back. If you lift stones to look underneath, replace them carefully – they arc someone's home.

Which shellfish hide under these holes in the sand?

The razor shell leaves two holes, very close together. **The cockle shell leaves two holes, slightly apart.** **The tellin leaves two holes, clearly separated.**

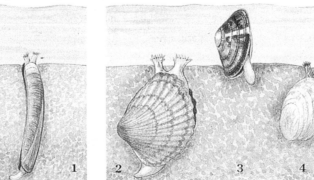

The razor shell, the cockle shell, the banded wedge and the tellin are all molluscs. Their shells have two halves.

What are caterpillars?

In spring you will see lots of caterpillars in the hedgerow.

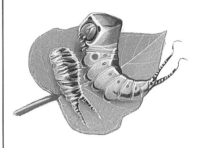

You will notice holes in the leaves where the caterpillars have been feeding. Most caterpillars feed on just one type of plant all their life. A caterpillar eats so much that eventually it becomes too fat to fit inside its skin. It splits its skin and wriggles out. Before it becomes a butterfly, the caterpillar will shed its skin several times. Most caterpillars moult, or shed their skin, five times, but some have as many as 17 moults. Finally the caterpillar changes into a chrysalis or pupa. The chrysalis stays still without moving or feeding until the butterfly is formed. This can take anything from 8 days to 4 years.

Agrias narcissus

■ Glossary

to Adapt: to change so as to become better suited to a habitat. Plant and animal species adapt over hundreds or even thousands of years.

Aquatic: we say a plant or animal is aquatic if it lives in or near water.

Bacteria: tiny one-celled organisms. They help to break down organic matter.

Brood: a group of young birds which have hatched at the same time from a single clutch of eggs.

Camouflage: the colour and patterns of an animal's skin or fur which help it to match its surroundings. Good camouflage protects prey from its predators.

Carnivore: meat-eater

to Colonize: to start up a community in a new place.

Community: a group of plants or animals growing or living together.

Deciduous: a tree is deciduous if it normally sheds its leaves each year.

to Dredge: to clean out a clogged pond, lake or river by scraping the bottom and sides. Waste material is taken away and dumped.

Ecosystem: a balanced combination of plants, animals, soil and climate. The different species have adapted to their habitat and to one another so that all can thrive.

to Erode: to wear away by the action of natural forces. Rain, wind, ice, rivers and sea water all erode the Earth's surface in different ways. Soil erosion can waste valuable land. The process of erosion is difficult to reverse.

Fertile: capable of supporting life and growth. A soil rich in nutrients is a fertile soil.

Food chain: in any community of plants and animals, there is a food chain. At the beginning of the chain will be the simplest plants; at the end of the food chain there may be large mammals. Each living thing depends on the others for its supply of food.

Gills: the organs in fish and other aquatic animals which enable them to breathe the oxygen they need to live.

Habitat: the natural home of a plant or an animal.

Herbivore: plant-eater

to Hibernate: to spend the winter, or most of it, asleep.

Humus: this rich material is formed as dead plants and leaves rot down. Humus on the forest floor feeds the soil which in turn feeds the plants and trees which are growing in the forest.

Krill: the tiny crustaceans which are in plankton, the food eaten by whales.

Leaf-mould: rotting leaves that will become humus.

to Migrate: to move from one place to another with the seasons. Many animals and birds migrate to find food or to mate and rear their young.

Minerals: inorganic substances occurring naturally in the Earth. Each has a specific chemical composition and distinctive physical characteristics.

Oxygen: a colourless, tasteless, odourless gas. It is present in air and in water. All plants and animals need oxygen to live.

Parasite: a plant or animal which lives on another plant or animal and takes its food directly from its host.

to Pollute: to make dirty. When natural habitats are polluted by industrial or human waste, the plants and animals that live there may be damaged or die.

Predator: an animal that hunts other animals for food.

Prey: an animal that is hunted for food.

Protected species: a species of animal or plant which you cannot harm or kill without breaking the law.

Seedling: a young plant which has been raised from a seed.

Siphon: a tube through which some molluscs take in food or push out waste. If the animal is buried in the sand, it can push its siphons to the surface.

to Spawn: to produce eggs or young. The word is used of fish and other aquatic creatures. The young themselves are also called spawn.

Species: a group of plants or animals whose members are closely related and can breed with each other.

to Stabilize: to make something stable, so that it will remain in a natural state of balance.

Sustainable resource: a resource which cannot be used up because it is renewed naturally.

Territory: an area of ground in which an animal and its family hunt or feed. Some animals mark the borders of their territory with scent or urine to warn off intruders.

Timber: name given to the wood of a tree. Much timber is pulped to make paper. Some is processed into tiny chips which

are used in many manufacturing industries. Timber which has been seasoned or dried out, can be used to make furniture, to build ships and houses, even to make musical instruments. Foresters shout the word "Timber!" to warn people that a tree is being felled.

Wetland: a marsh or swamp, or other area of damp land. Wetlands support a rich variety of plant and animal species. Many of the Earth's wetlands are threatened by land reclamation and building projects, but many are also now protected.

THE COUNTRYSIDE CODE

- Guard against fire:
  don't drop matches, paper or glass.

- Fasten gates:
  they are there to keep animals in or out.

- Keep dogs under control:
  they can frighten and hurt farm animals
  and flatten crops.

- Keep to public paths across farmland:
  humans can scare animals and damage crops too.

- Use gates and stiles to cross walls and fences:
  they are there to prevent wear and tear to
  the fences and to help you cross safely.

- Take your litter home:
  litter looks ugly, pollutes the environment
  and can be dangerous to animals.

- Keep watercourses clean:
  never drop anything into ponds, lakes or rivers.

- Don't pick or damage plants:
  they may be rare or protected species.

- Don't make unnecessary noise:
  other people and animals need peace and quiet
  in the countryside.

**The Countryside Code was devised by
the Countryside Commission.**

COUNTRY WALKS

You can find out more about walking and rambling
in Britain if you contact:

The National Trust
36 Queen Anne's Gate
London SW1

WATCH
(Junior branch of RSNC)
The Green
Witham Park
Waterside South
Lincoln

Young Ornithologists Club
RSPB, Junior Branch
The Lodge
Sandy
Bedfordshire

Ramblers' Association
1/5 Wandsworth Road
London SW8

Definitive footpaths are shown on the Landranger
series of Ordnance Survey maps.

INDEX

The entries in **bold** refer to whole chapters on the subject.